HIBERNIAN
18 75
EDINBURGH

THE OFFICIAL
HIBERNIAN
FOOTBALL CLUB
ANNUAL 2025

Written by Richard Payne
Designed by Lucy Boyd

g

A Grange Publication

© 2024. Published by Grange Communications Ltd., Edinburgh, under licence from Hibernian Football Club.

Printed in the EU.

Photographs @ Hibernian Football Club

Special thanks to Alan Rennie and Cameron Allan.

ISBN 978-1-915879-87-5

CONTENTS

WELCOME

A very warm welcome to the latest edition of The Official Hibernian Football Club Annual!

As ever, it is packed with interviews and features to take you behind the scenes at Easter Road.

We'll look back on an eventful season last term that included a memorable European campaign, and we look forward to David Gray's first season in charge of the Club.

We take a close look at this season's squads and chat to our 2024 Player of the Year – Jordan Obita – about his time at the Club so far.

New signing Kirsten Reilly tells us about her love for the Club and why she has returned to Hibs for a second spell.

We discuss the wider Hibernian family and the ongoing initiatives from the Hibernian Community Foundation during these testing times.

We'll speak to Derek White about his role at the Club and how he balances his work between the men's and women's teams. We also chat to Rory Whittaker about his remarkable rise to prominence last term and his ambitions going forward.

We'll test your Hibee knowledge with quizzes and look back on one of the Club's most famous European ties – when we defeated the mighty Barcelona in 1960/61.

We also have all your usual favourites and much more to keep you up to date with the Club you love.

Glory, Glory to the Hibees!

2023/24 SEASON REVIEW

JUNE

The close season proved to be a time of change for the Club both on and off the field. We welcomed goalkeepers Max Boruc and Jojo Wollacott, defender Jordan Obita, and forward Adam Le Fondre. Following the departure of Dean Gibson as manager of the women's team, we appointed Grant Scott as his successor. The new boss returned to the Club for a second spell, having previously brought success to the Hibees, and wasted little time in reshaping his squad. Tegan Bowie, Abbie Ferguson, Katie Fraine and Mya Christie joined us whilst experienced duo Ellis Notley and Joelle Murray earned new deals. Gareth Evans was appointed as Academy Director, Darren McGregor became the Under-18 Coach, whilst Guillaume Beuzelin became the Club's new Academy Head of Coaching. June also saw players, staff and supporters come together for the Ron Gordon 24-hour football challenge at the Club's training centre. The event saw a football match played continuously over a 24-hour period and raised substantial funds for the Hibernian Community Foundation, allowing the Club's official charity to provide community lunches from the stadium for a whole year!

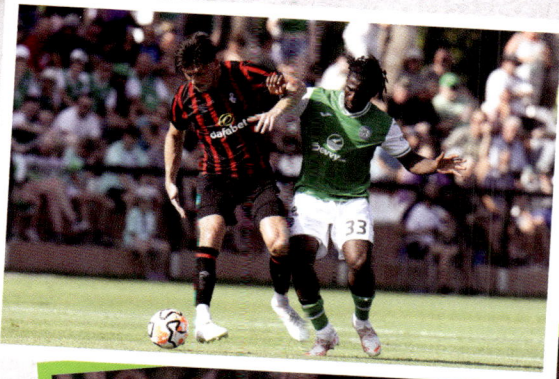

JULY

There was further player movement for both the men's and women's teams. The men recruited Dylan Vente, Will Fish, Riley Harbottle and Dylan Levitt. Paul Hanlon was once again named as the team captain. Hibs Women were active in the market as well signing Naomi Powell, Nina Wilson and Loran Doran-Barr. There were new deals for Kirsty Morrison and Shannon Leishman as the women headed to Ireland for their pre-season training camp before hosting a friendly with Newcastle United on their return. The men's pre-season offered a mix bag of results with victories over Edinburgh City, FC Europa and FC Groningen and defeats from encounters with AFC Bournemouth and Blackpool. The competitive action started with a trip to Andorra in the second qualifying round of the UEFA Europa Conference League. Sadly, we were to suffer a 2-1 defeat to Inter Club d'Escaldes.

AUGUST

The return leg at Easter Road started with a series of goalkeeping issues with David Marshall injured during the warm-up whilst his replacement, Wollacott, also suffered an injury just minutes into his debut. Young goalkeeper Boruc was handed a baptism of fire and performed admirably in his first outing as we hit Inter Club d'Escaldes for six. Martin Boyle notched a brace on his return to competitive action following a lengthy lay-off. We then faced Swiss Super League opponents FC Luzern and produced a stunning performance to win 3-1. The return in Luzern was every bit as memorable as we progressed 5-3 on aggregate after drawing 2-2. Elie Youan and Boyle both scored on a famous night in Switzerland. That meant we were into the Play-Off against English giants Aston Villa. Their Premier League class proved a step too far for our boys and we lost 5-0 on John McGinn's return to Easter Road. Our European adventure came at a cost to our league form as we lost our opening three fixtures. Boss Lee Johnston was dismissed and replaced in the interim by David Gray. Our Under-18s defeated Hearts 1-0 in the wee derby before thrashing Celtic 5-0. Rudi Molotnikov penned a new three-year deal whilst the Club revealed striker Harry McKirdy would be missing for a significant period following successful heart surgery. Hibs Women collected their first win of the season with a 4-1 win over Montrose before staging a dramatic fightback against Spartans as Brooke Nunn scored an incredible injury time equaliser.

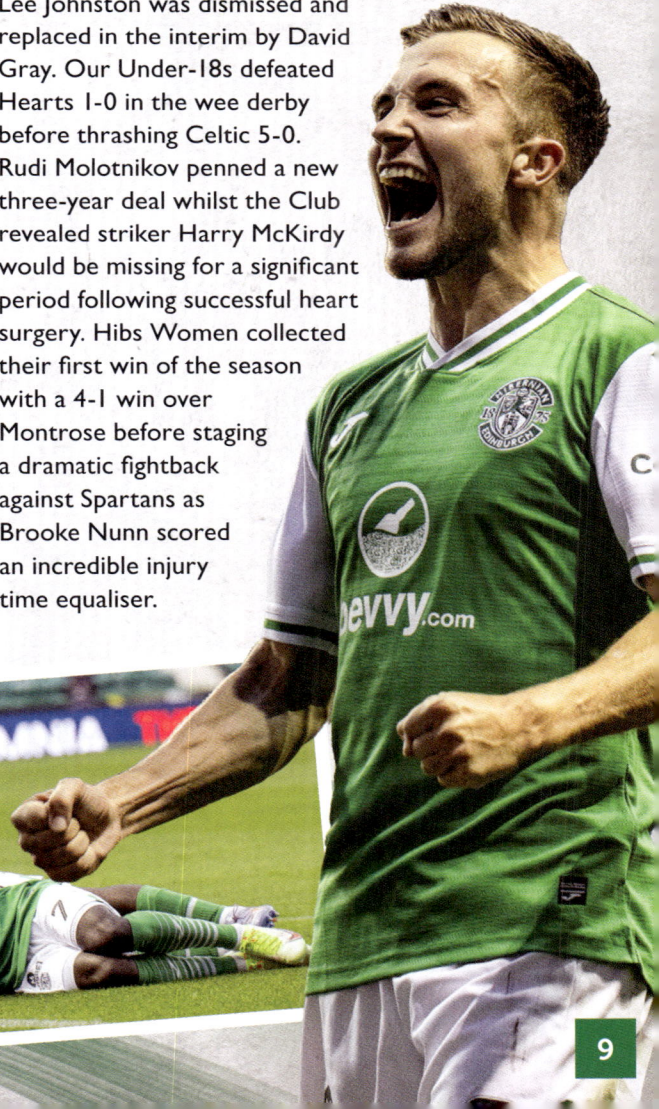

SEPTEMBER

Gray's third tenure as caretaker boss included an impressive with over Aberdeen at Pittodrie thanks to goals from substitutes, Christian Doidge and Le Fondre. After the match, Nick Montgomery would be appointed our new head coach. His tenure would begin with a draw at Rugby Park against Kilmarnock as the hosts fought back late on to snatch a share of the spoils. One week later, Montgomery claimed his first win as Hibs boss with a 2-0 victory over St Johnstone thanks to goals from Lewis Miller and Dylan Vente. Rory Whittaker becomes the Club's youngest-ever player at 16 years and 44 days. Storm Agnes couldn't stop us progressing after a Viaplay Cup thriller against St Mirren under our newly installed LED floodlights. Hibs Women continue their turnaround in fortunes under Grant Scott by winning the Capital Cup after defeating Hearts 1-0 at Tynecastle. Shannon McGregor celebrates her 100th appearance for the Club by scoring in a 5-0 win over Aberdeen. Jorian Baucom scored a hat-trick in that game and continued her impressive scoring start to life in green and white when she scored the only goal of the game against Motherwell. After a string of impressive performances, defender Poppy Lawson was rewarded with a contract extension until 2026.

OCTOBER

October began with the news that Allan Delferrière had signed a new three-year deal to remain at the Club. We would draw three of our four fixtures during the month against Hearts, Celtic and Ross County. The draw against the Jambos at Tynecastle was the most impressive as Elie Youan struck twice in a little over one minute when we battled back from 2-0 down to claim an unlikely point. Skipper Paul Hanlon became only the fifth player to reach 550 appearances for the Club during our defeat against Rangers in Philippe Clement's first match in charge of the Ibrox men. Miller's impressive displays earnt the defender a call up for the Australian national side and he would pick up his first cap against England at Wembley Stadium. October also saw the highly anticipated testimonial match for 'Sir' David Gray. The main man himself notched the only goal of the game against a Manchester United XI as a host of former Hibs players pulled on the famous green jersey one more time. Eilidh Adams celebrated her first senior hat-trick in an 8-1 win over Hamilton Academical by signing a contract extension until 2026.

NOVEMBER

Despite a strong performance from the boys, we would suffer heartache at Hampden Park as Bojan Miovski struck an ill-deserved winner for Aberdeen to dump us out of the League Cup. Our defensive frailties were again exposed as St Mirren snatched an injury time equaliser in Paisley as we dropped two points on the road. We would get back to winning ways as Josh Campbell scored the only goal of the game in a narrow victory over Kilmarnock on Remembrance Day. The men would finish the month strongly by defeating Dundee 2-1 at Dens Park thanks to a stunning team goal finished off by the rejuvenated Jair Tavares and a powerful header by Miller, who would later be sent off. Youngster Josh Landers was the latest to commit his future to the Club when he put pen to paper on a new three-year deal. Hibs Women continued to score goals for fun during November with Ferguson notching four goals in an 8-0 victory away to Montrose before Adams notched her second hat-trick in three games after celebrating her 100th appearance for the Club during a 7-0 thrashing of Dundee United. The girls lifted silverware for the second time this season by retaining the Capital Cup with a 2-1 victory over Hearts at Easter Road in front of 5,365 fans. Baucom scored both goals whilst Leah Eddie lifted the trophy after skippering the team and becoming the latest player to reach a century of appearances for the Club.

DECEMBER

Vente and Fish scored the crucial goals as Aberdeen's profligacy came back to bite them. Marshall saved Bojan Miovski's penalty kick in a game that saw the Dons hit the post twice. Doidge netted our only goal in a 4-1 defeat to champions Celtic before we bounced back with a win away to Livingston thanks to Boyle's goal. Boyle would make his 300th appearance for the Club during December. The year ended with defeats from St Johnstone and Hearts. Hibs Women were impressive and they thrashed Aberdeen 7-0 with Baucom netting her second hat-trick of the campaign.

JANUARY

We welcomed in the New Year with a home match against Motherwell. Youan's late equaliser saw us snatch a point late on. The boys then travelled to Dubai for a mid-season training camp, which included a friendly against Swiss team, Servette. Afterwards, we returned home to face plucky Forfar Athletic in the Scottish Cup. Doidge scored the only goal of the game – his final for the Club. We saw big changes during January to our squad with the arrivals of Nathan Moriah-Welsh, Luke Amos, Myziane Maolida, Owen Bevan, Emiliano Marcondes, Nectarios Triantis and Eliezer Mayenda. Jimmy Jeggo left for Melbourne City, Doidge went to Forest Green Rovers and several youngsters went out on loan. It was goal galore for Hibs Women as Grant Scott's side thrashed St Johnstone 10-0, Hamilton, 4-0, Motherwell 5-0 and Dundee United 4-0.

FEBRUARY

Having made so many changes to the team in the winter transfer window, it was always going to take time for the boys to gel, and consequently, February opened with back-to-back defeats to St Mirren and Celtic at Easter Road. Thereafter, our results started to improve, beginning with a Scottish Cup win in the Highlands against Inverness Caledonian Thistle. We would then draw with Aberdeen and Heart of Midlothian on the road, either side of a home win against Dundee. Hibs Women took the scalp of old rivals Glasgow City by knocking them out of the Scottish Cup in spot kicks after a draw at Petershill Park.

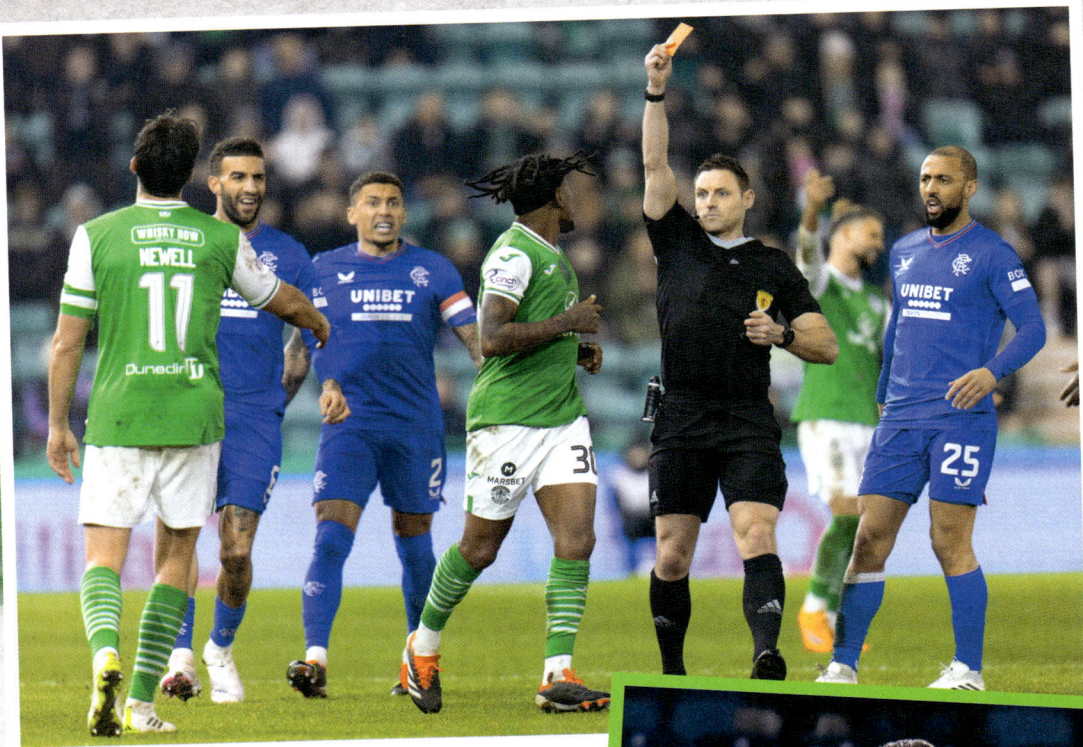

MARCH

We took our good form into March and a 2-0 home victory over Ross County pushed us into the top six of the cinch Premiership. A Hibs XI faced Raith Rovers in Lewis Vaughan's testimonial match and won 5-1 in Kirkcaldy, with Lewis Stevenson and Hanlon both scoring against their future employers. We were then on the wrong end of some controversial VAR decisions as red cards for Obita and Moriah-Welsh cost us dearly as we exited the Scottish Cup before dropping crucial league points against Ross County due to an injury time leveller. We produced one of our best performances of the season to defeat relegation-threatened Livingston 3-0 to keep alive our top-six hopes. The month ends with Murray making a landmark 500th appearance for Hibs Women in a match against Rangers at Broadwood.

APRIL

Our top-six hopes take a knock when we suffer defeat in the penultimate match before the split as St Johnstone leave Easter Road with all three points following a disappointing afternoon. One week later and our bottom-six place is confirmed as Motherwell scored an ill-deserved equaliser at the death to cancel out Myziane's opener. Midfielder Campbell made his 100th appearances for the Club. Eddie and Baucom are both named in the PFA SWPL Team of the Year. Darren McGregor's U18 side defeat Celtic 4-1 and Rangers 3-2 – the victory over the Ibrox side is the third time the boys had beaten them this season. After the international break, the senior side take full points from our first post-split fixture as goals from Emiliano, Hanlon and Vente earn a 3-1 win away to St Johnstone. Emiliano's stunning free kick would be voted our Goal of the Season. Josh O'Connor, Kanayo Megwa and Murray Aiken – all on loan to Airdrieonians – help the Diamonds to lift the SPFL Trust Trophy for the first time in 15 years with victory over Welsh outfit, The New Saints.

MAY

Hibs Women finish the season strongly, coming from 2-0 down away to Glasgow City to snatch a point at the death before the girls beat city rivals Hearts for the third time this season. Aberdeen's biggest win in Leith for almost four decades proves to be Montgomery's last game in charge as he is dismissed in the aftermath of the contest. Gray takes interim charge before being appointed permanently to the role during the summer. May also proved to be an emotional month for the Club as a trio of long-term servants departed the Club. Stevenson and Hanlon play their final home match for the Club as we romp to a comfortable 3-0 victory over Motherwell, with Stevenson marking the occasion by reaching his 600th appearance. Elsewhere, Murray makes her 507th and final appearance for the Club and leaves the field to a guard of honour from both teams at Celtic Park.

15

PLAYER
PROFILES

POSITION: GOALKEEPER

JOSEF
BURSIK

Josef joined us during the summer on a season-long loan from Club Brugge in Belgium. The English shot-stopper arrived in Leith with a wealth of experience at both domestic and international level. His former clubs include AFC Wimbledon, Stoke City, Doncaster Rovers, Peterborough United and Lincoln City. He has represented England at several youth levels.

POSITION: GOALKEEPER

JORDAN
SMITH

Jordan, like Josef, joined the Club during the summer. The shot-stopper has featured predominantly in the English Championship during his career — making 47 league appearances for Nottingham Forest whilst also spending time out on loan at Barnsley, Mansfield Town, and Huddersfield Town before joining Stockport County in July 2023. He is contracted to the Club until the summer of 2026.

POSITION: GOALKEEPER

MAX BORUC

The young goalkeeper was thrown into the deep end when he made his debut just 19 minutes into our Europa Conference League qualifier against Inter Club d'Escaldes following injuries to David Marshall and Jojo Wollacott. Max started his career with Swedish side Husqvarna FF before spells in England with Stoke City and West Bromwich Albion. He joined us from Śląsk Wrocław.

POSITION: DEFENDER

LEWIS MILLER

The full back was a figure of consistency last season and his performances saw him rewarded with a call-up to the Australian national side. He made his debut for the Socceroos against England at a packed Wembley Stadium. The former Central Coast Mariners defender is now in his third season at the Club, having made his debut against Clyde in the League Cup back in 2022.

POSITION: DEFENDER

MARVIN EKPITETA

Towering centre back Ekpiteta joined us this summer on a three-year deal following the expiration of his contract with English League One outfit Blackpool. Marvin rose through the English pyramid, winning promotion with both Leyton Orient and Blackpool. A firm fans' favourite with the Seasiders, he won their Player of the Year and Players' Player of the Year awards in 2022.

POSITION: DEFENDER

WARREN O'HORA

Former Republic of Ireland youth international O'Hora put pen to paper on a three-year deal with us this summer. He made his professional debut for Bohemians before making the switch to Brighton and Hove Albion in the English Premier League. He was loaned to MK Dons in 2020 before making the move permanent, and it was here that most of his senior appearances came.

POSITION: DEFENDER

CHRIS CADDEN

Chris missed most of last term after rupturing his Achilles tendon during the final game of the 2022/23 campaign. He returned to the side towards the end of last season and made 13 appearances, scoring once. The former Motherwell and Columbus Crew defender has two Scotland caps after appearances against Peru and Mexico back in 2018.

POSITION: DEFENDER

JORDAN OBITA

Jordan was a stand-out performer during his first season in Leith and scooped the Club's Player of the Year and Players' Player of the Year awards. The former Wycombe Wanderers defender's highlights from last term include scoring a pivotal goal against FC Luzern in the dying moments shortly after joining the Club. The former England youth international is comfortable playing either at left back or left wing.

POSITION: DEFENDER

KANAYO MEGWA

Kanayo joined us in 2021 and was a stand-out performer as part of Gareth Evans' U18 side that won the CAS Elite Youth League and competed brilliantly in the UEFA Youth League, where he came up against Molde FK, FC Nantes, and Borussia Dortmund. Megwa scooped our 2023 Academy Player of the Year award and made his senior debut vs Motherwell in August of the same year.

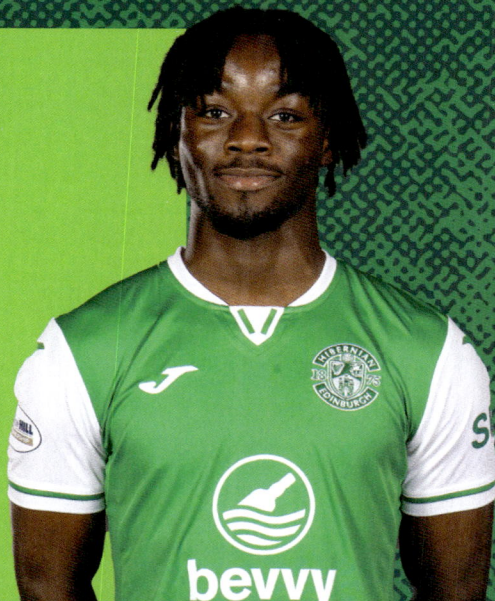

POSITION: DEFENDER

ROCKY BUSHIRI

The powerful and intimidating defender joined us initially on a six-month loan from Norwich City in January 2022. He was raw and unpolished; however, the Club saw enough potential to make the move permanent. Since then, Rocky has grown into a reliable and consistent performer. He made 35 appearances last season, and despite going close on several occasions, he has yet to break his scoring duck.

POSITION: DEFENDER

JACK IREDALE

In summer 2024 we moved to bring in the experienced defender on a two-year deal. The centre-back joined us from English League One side Bolton Wanderers, whom he helped to reach the English League One Play-Off Final at Wembley Stadium in 2023/24. Jack has amassed over 250 senior appearances during his career and has been capped by Australia at youth level.

POSITION: MIDFIELDER

DYLAN LEVITT

The Welsh international arrived from Dundee United last season. Dylan came through the youth ranks at Manchester United before gaining experience whilst on loan at Charlton Athletic and Croatian side Istra 1961. Levitt was part of the Wales World Cup squad in 2022.

POSITION: MIDFIELDER

JAKE DOYLE-HAYES

Irishman Doyle-Hayes has been with us since the summer of 2021; however, last season will have unquestionably been his most frustrating after injury limited him to just 257 minutes on the pitch throughout the whole campaign. He did manage to feature against his former Club, Aston Villa, in the Europa Conference League Play-Offs. The industrious midfielder can either play a holding role or box to box.

POSITION: MIDFIELDER

JOE NEWELL

The classy midfielder is an influential figure on and off the field and is a leader within our dressing room. The 31-year-old was named Club Captain due to his leadership capabilities, following the departure of Paul Hanlon. Joe is a fierce competitor and his composure on the ball during the heat of battle is what sets him apart from his opponents. He signed a new deal during the summer keeping him at Easter Road until 2027.

POSITION: MIDFIELDER

LUKE AMOS

Luke joined the Club in January 2024 after a successful trial period. The former England youth international is a product of the Tottenham Hotspur Academy and spent 14 years with Spurs working his way through the age groups. He benefited from loan spells, including a stint with Queens Park Rangers, whom he impressed so much they made the move permanent.

POSITION: MIDFIELDER

HYEOKKYU KWON

Kwon, a defensive midfielder, joined us during the summer, and in doing so, he became the first South Korean to play for the Club. The 23-year-old arrived from fellow Scottish Premiership side Celtic on loan for the duration of this campaign. Hyeok-kyu initially joined the Hoops on a five-year deal in the summer of 2023 from K-League 2 outfit Busan Park and spent part of last season with St Mirren.

POSITION: MIDFIELDER

NICKY CADDEN

Nicky penned a three-year deal with the Club during the summer, joining his twin brother Chris at the Club. He has made over 350 senior appearances to date and has experience of the Scottish game through spells with Airdrieonians, Livingston, Ayr United and Greenock Morton. The winger won the English League Two title with Forest Green Rovers before two years with Barnsley in League One.

POSITION: MIDFIELDER

NOHAN KENNEH

Kenneh joined us in the summer of 2022 from Leeds United on a three-year-deal. A combative player, Nohan has struggled to break into the side and has spent time on loan with Ross County and Shrewsbury Town to obtain game time. Kenneh's versatility means that he can play in either defence or midfield.

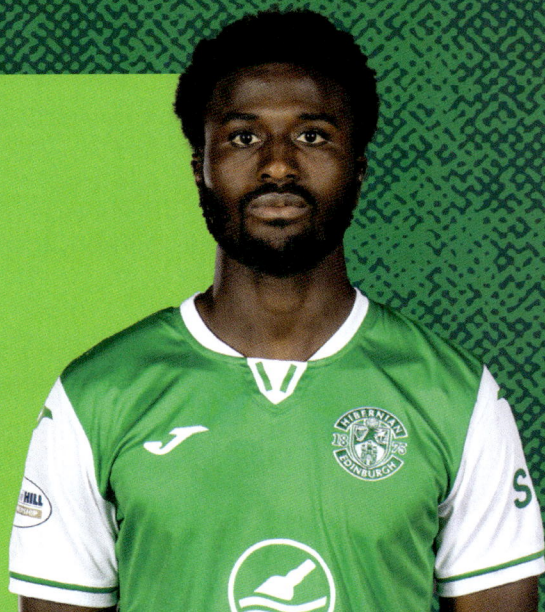

POSITION: MIDFIELDER

NECTARIOS TRIANTIS

The combative Australian returned to Hibs on deadline day in summer 2024, joining on a season-long loan move from English Championship outfit Sunderland. The 21-year-old made 14 appearances for us last term across all competitions, primarily as a defender, however he has been brought back as a defensive midfielder. Triantis has been capped by the Socceroos at under-23 level.

POSITION: MIDFIELDER

NATHAN MORIAH-WELSH

Despite only arriving during the winter transfer window, Moriah-Welsh did enough during his 16 appearances last term to scoop our Young Player of the Year award. The 22-year-old Guyana international joined us from AFC Bournemouth on a deal until 2026. Tidy in possession, he is energetic and combative, often doing an overlooked role in the middle of the park.

POSITION: MIDFIELDER

JOSH CAMPBELL

The Academy graduate suffered an injury-disrupted season last term; however, he did still manage to score five times in 27 appearances. A boyhood Hibee, Campbell was a league and cup winner with us at under-18 level, and he would love nothing more than clinching silverware for the Club at a senior level. Josh made his 100th appearance for the Club during last season.

POSITION: MIDFIELDER

RUDI MOLOTNIKOV

Whilst making his senior debut last season against Aston Villa, it wasn't until the summer when the young academy graduate broke into the first team on a regular basis. Starting all four of our Premier Sports Cup group matches, 18-year-old Rudi impressed in each and netted in the games against Queen's Park and Peterhead. Molotnikov spent part of last season on loan with Stirling Albion to gain first team experience.

POSITION: FORWARD

ELIE YOUAN

The classy Frenchman is blessed with blistering pace and no shortage of tricks up his sleeves, Youan is a handful for any defence. After initially joining us on a season-long loan from Swiss club, St Gallen, we took up the option to buy after a series of impressive performances from Élie. The winger scored nine times in 43 appearances last term and contributed several assists.

POSITION: FORWARD

MARTIN BOYLE

Martin remains a talismanic figure in our side and has enjoyed a long and prolific time in Leith. A firm fans' favourite, Boyle was part of our 2016 Scottish Cup and 2017 Championship winning sides. Now an established Australian international, he continues to contribute for the Club and finished last term joint-top goal scorer alongside Myziane Maolida, with 11 goals.

POSITION: FORWARD

HARRY MCKIRDY

The English forward missed a significant portion of last season due to a serious health issue, and once he returned, he spent time on loan to Swindon Town. It was familiar surroundings for Harry following a prolific spell with the Robins during the 2021/22 season that ironically secured his move to Easter Road. McKirdy's former clubs also include Aston Villa, Stoke City, Port Vale, Carlisle United, Newport County, Crewe, and Stevenage.

POSITION: FORWARD

KIERON BOWIE

Kirkcaldy-born Bowie first came to the attention of the Scottish football public when he burst onto the scene with his hometown club, Raith Rovers. He would help the Stark's Park men clinch the League One title and promotion to the Championship before joining Fulham in 2020. The Scotland youth international helped Northampton Town win promotion to League One in England during a loan spell with The Cobblers. He joined us on a four-year deal back in August.

POSITION: FORWARD

JUNIOR HOILETT

Experienced Canadian international Hoilett brings a wealth of experience to a young Hibs team. The 34-year-old has over 500 career appearances to date after spells with Blackburn Rovers, St. Pauli, Queens Park Rangers, Cardiff City, Reading and Vancouver White Caps amongst others. Junior spent the latter part of last season with Aberdeen, where he contributed to 10 goals (eight assists, two goals) in 15 appearances.

POSITION: FORWARD

MYKOLA KUHAREVICH

The powerful Ukrainian striker returned to bolster our attack on a season-long loan from English Championship outfit Swansea City. Mykola made a big impression following a short stint with us during the 2022/23 campaign, where he scored five times in 15 appearances. The 23-year-old is a Ukrainian youth international and has experience of playing in Belgium, France, and England, as well as his home nation.

WHO AM I?

GO TO P60-61 FOR THE ANSWERS

Can you figure out who the four mystery Hibees are?

01

I started my career with Motherwell.

My brother is also a professional footballer.

I joined Hibs from Columbus Crew in the MLS.

I won the Club's Player of the Year award in my first full season with Hibs.

I have two Scotland caps from matches against Peru and Mexico in 2018.

ANSWER:

02

I was born in Tamworth, England.

I joined Hibs from Rotherham United in 2019.

I won the Players' Player of the Year and Player of the Year awards in 2023.

I made my Hibs debut against Stirling Albion in the 2019 League Cup at Forthbank Stadium.

Last season I was cautioned more than any other Hibs player.

ANSWER:

03

I am a Hibs supporter and won a league and cup double with the U18s.

I scored twice against Inter Club d'Escaldes in the Europa Conference League qualifiers at Easter Road.

I made my 100th appearance for the Club against Motherwell on the final fixture before the league split.

Before making my breakthrough at Hibs, I was on loan to Airdrieonians, Arbroath and Edinburgh City.

I won the Young Player of the Year award in 2023 as well as winning Goal of the Season for an injury time equaliser against Rangers.

ANSWER:

04

I came through the Club's youth academy to realise my dream of playing for Hibs.

I made my debut aged 16 against Hamilton Academical in the Women's Scottish Cup.

I made my 100th appearance for the Club during last season's 7-0 victory over Dundee United in the SWPL Cup.

I marked this occasion by scoring a hat-trick whilst skippering the side too.

I missed a large part of last season through injury.

ANSWER:

SEASON 2023/24 IN STATS

→ **MEN**
→ **WOMEN**

BIGGEST WIN

6-1 VS INTER CLUB D'ESCALDES, EUROPA CONFERENCE LEAGUE, 2ND ROUND QUALIFIER, 2ND LEG

10-0 VS ST. JOHNSTONE, SCOTTISH CUP, 3RD ROUND

TOTAL GOALS CONCEDED
80 / 58

TOTAL GOALS SCORED
75 / 97

OWN GOALS RECEIVED
2 / 4

HAT-TRICKS
0 / 6

PENALTY KICKS RECEIVED
6 / 7

TOP GOAL SCORER
MARTIN BOYLE & MYZIANE MAOLIDA, 11
JORIAN BAUCOM, 28

FINAL LEAGUE POSITION
8TH / 5TH

MOST APPEARANCES
JOE NEWELL, 49
POPPY LAWSON & JORIAN BAUCOM, 38

MOST CAUTIONED
JOE NEWELL, 12
POPPY LAWSON, 7

OWN GOALS CONCEDED
4 / 0

NUMBER OF RED CARDS RECEIVED
3 / 2

CLEAN SHEETS
11 / 13

NUMBER OF YELLOW CARDS RECEIVED
90 / 41

PENALTY KICKS CONCEDED
12 / 2

MOST MINUTES PLAYED
JOE NEWELL, 4,083
POPPY LAWSON, 3,272

DAVID GRAY: THE TIME IS NOW

After four separate stints as interim Head Coach, David Gray felt the time was right to make the position his own.

Our Scottish Cup-winning captain has spent over a decade with the Club – seven as a player and three as a coach – and he knows better than anyone what it takes to bring success to Hibs, having seen it at close hand.

Gray has assembled a backroom team that, like him, understand our Club and the high demands that are set and expected.

Eddie May, Liam Craig and Craig Samson have all been over the course before at Hibs and their strengths and weaknesses complement Gray's.

David, who accepted the position whilst on a long-awaited and much deserved family holiday in Florida, admits everything he has been through over the last few years has been building to this appointment.

He said: "Everyone is well aware of how much this Club means to me. I've had great times here.

"Now that I'm sitting in this position, I look back to the very first time I was asked to lead the team (League Cup Final in 2021 vs Celtic).

Hibernian Training Centre
Main Entrance

I want us to be aggressive in terms of the intensity all the time. I want us to attack as an eleven and defend as one too.

"Had we won that game, and I was then asked to take over, would that have been the right thing to do? Absolutely not.

"The progression I've made in the last three years since then has been geared towards now. I wanted the job. That was the most important thing. I had done four interim periods.

"I felt this was the right time to go and make a difference here, to put myself out there and apply for the job properly.

"What I've learned is there is more than one way to play. Every single manager has brought their own style, everyone has their own ways of working.

"I think I've been gathering all this information over the time, being in a position to take the good parts, see what maybe didn't work, and put them together in what a successful Hibs team should look like."

Having been part of previous coaching staffs and due to his four stints as interim Head Coach, Gray believes he knows what it takes to get our Club challenging once again.

He has called on his players to embrace being here and meeting the demands of playing for such a big and historic Club as ours.

Gray commented: "There was no need for any introductions because I knew every single player inside out. I knew their strengths and their weaknesses, and it was the same with the staff.

"I feel I have added to that with the staff I have assembled around me. Every one of them has worked here before or were currently working here and they know what the Club is all about.

"We are part of a fantastic club and, when things are going well, it can be the best place to play football.

"There are challenges that come when playing for Hibs because of the expectation that is there, and rightly so, because we have an amazing club, fantastic fanbase, amazing facilities, and that comes with certain demands.

"We need to make sure that the players are aware of that at all times but not to be intimidated by it, rather to embrace it, because like I said, this can be one of the best places to be."

Gray himself played through a relatively successful period for the Club and he admits the target for us every year should be to claim a trophy and European qualification.

"I want us to be aggressive in terms of the intensity all the time. I want us to attack as an 11 and defend as one too.

"Look, at the start of every season our goal is to win a trophy and qualify for Europe. Is that a realistic target? Absolutely. I've managed to live that and breathe that myself.

"The fans deserve it, they crave it. The players were made aware on day one that, when we're goal setting for the season, we need realistic targets – and that's exactly what it is.

"Every expectation on this Hibs team must be trying to win a trophy – and to finish in a European position. That's the aim from the start of the season."

2023/24 SEASON QUIZ

1. Hibernian Women recorded the Club's biggest win of the season. Who was it against and what was the score?

2. Who did Hibernian defeat to claim our first win of the Premiership campaign?

3. How many clean sheets did David Marshall keep in all competitions?

4. Which Hibernian player was red carded just 21 minutes into her debut?

5. Lewis Miller made his international debut for Australia last season. Who were the Socceroos' opponents that night?

6. Myziane Maolida joined Hibs on loan from which German team?

7. Can you name the four players to score a hat-trick for the Club last season?

8. Elie Youan scored a quick-fire brace against Hearts last season as we came from behind to secure a share of the spoils. How many seconds were between his two goals?

9. How many games did the men draw 2-2 last season in all competitions?

10. When Rory Whittaker made his debut for the Club last season, he became our youngest ever player at 16 years and 44 days old. Who previously held that record?

11. Lia Tweedie scored Hibs Women's Goal of the Season. Who were our opponents that day?

12. How many goals did Women's top goal scorer, Jorian Baucom, net in all competitions?

13. Lewis Stevenson made his 600th and final appearance for the Club against which opponent?

14. Which Hibs player received the most yellow cards last season?

15. Who won the Men's Player of the Year and Player's Player of the Year awards?

GO TO P60-61 FOR THE ANSWERS

2024 PLAYER OF THE YEAR AWARDS

Defender Jordan Obita brought the curtain down on his first season in Edinburgh by deservedly walking off with two awards at the Club's Player of the Year event.

Obita was a stand-out performer throughout last season and was a thoroughly deserving recipient of the Men's Player of the Year and Player's Player of the Year awards.

He was a virtual ever-present during a challenging campaign, making 44 appearances and scoring twice.

Nonetheless, his contribution and tireless effort were greatly appreciated by the fans and his team-mates alike as they voted for Jordan as their Player of the Year.

Reflecting on his first season in green and white, he said: "I really enjoyed my first season with the Club, and it felt good to win both awards.

"Being voted for by the fans and my team-mates meant they are special awards, and I was very grateful to have won them.

"Everyone has been brilliant with me since I first arrived at the Club. I love playing for this team and hopefully there is a lot more to come."

Elsewhere, Nathan Moriah-Welsh scooped the Men's Young Player of the Year award, despite having only joined us during the winter transfer window.

Moriah-Welsh made 15 appearances after making the switch from AFC Bournemouth and immediately became a fixture of our midfield

engine room where his combative approach and composure on the ball made him an asset.

Reflecting on his award, Nathan commented: "It was a bit unexpected to be honest but I'm really happy to receive it."

"It was a tough season for the team collectively but a good learning experience for me. I felt I came in and made a positive adjustment to the team."

Meanwhile, Leah Eddie collected the Women's Player of the Year award following an outstanding campaign in which she forced her way into the national side.

Eddie's award was voted for by her peers who recognised her contribution during the season –

her fifth and final campaign with the Club before moving to Rangers during the summer.

Lia Tweedie picked up the second award of the evening for the girls by winning the Women's Goal of the Season for her incredible finish against city rivals Heart of Midlothian.

Joelle Murray, who called time on her remarkable career during the close season, received a Special Recognition Award for her services to Hibernian FC.

Finally, Rory Whittaker won the Academy Player of the Year award, Emiliano Marcondes won the Men's Goal of the season for his stunning free kick against St Johnstone and Facilities Manager Rab Dunn was recognised by his peers as the Staff Member of the Year.

THE 2024 AWARD WINNERS

Men's Player of the Year
Jordan Obita

Men's Players' Player of the Year
Jordan Obita

Women's Goal of the Season
Lia Tweedie vs Hearts

Women's Player of the Year
Leah Eddie

Special Recognition Award
Joelle Murray

Academy Player of the Year
Rory Whittaker

Men's Young Player of the Year
Nathan Moriah-Welsh

Men's Goal of the Season
Emiliano Marcondes vs St Johnstone

Staff Member of the Year
Rab Dunn (Facilities Manager)

DEVELOPMENT

There is nothing more precarious as potential and the Club take their responsibility of nurturing and developing talent seriously.

Last season no fewer than six youngsters were given the opportunity to make their first team debuts – Rory Whittaker, Rudi Molotnikov, Reuben McAllister, Kanayo Megwa, Josh Landers and Jacob MacIntyre all made their senior bows.

Each deserved their promotion, however the Club have been careful to bleed the youngsters in over time and not overwhelm them.

Yet, the rise of Whittaker caught the attention more than most after he became the Club's youngest-ever player when he stepped off the bench against St Johnstone at 16 years and 44 days old.

The right back made an immediate impression and racked up 14 senior appearances last term before rounding off a remarkable campaign by scooping the Academy Player of the Year Award at the Club's end of season ceremony.

Whittaker, who joined us from Spartans aged just nine, also forced his way into the Scotland U19 set-up too.

Yet, he knows that if he is to follow recent Academy graduates Josh Doig and Ryan Porteous by establishing themselves in the Hibs and then hopefully the Scotland senior side, then the hard work is only just starting.

Rory's fantastic attitude and humility means that he is acutely aware of this as he reflected on his achievements so far: "All the coaches made it clear that I'm at the start of my journey and my debut was just the first milestone.

"I've approached this season with the same mindset and attitude as last, work hard and take it from there."

Whittaker's debut appearance saw him break Jamie McCluskey's near 20-year record as our youngest-ever player and a signalled meteoric rise to prominence for the defender who had just weeks earlier been a ball boy.

He recalled: "Everything happened so quickly. A month before, the Academy lads were ball boys for the European games, and it never crossed my mind I would be on the pitch making my debut so soon after!

"I was nervous the day before the St Johnstone game because I knew I was in the squad, and I

"It was a dream come true to make my debut. It will be something that I will always look back on with great pride."

remember talking to my dad about it all before going to bed. I woke up the next morning and the nerves had turned to excitement.

"It was a dream come true to make my debut. It will be something that I will always look back on with great pride."

His performances saw him rewarded with a new three-year deal, and come the end of the season the young defender was becoming more accustomed to lining up alongside his boyhood heroes.

"It was surreal to start with because I have always been a Hibs fan and for years had looked up to the likes of Paul Hanlon and Lewis Stevenson as my heroes, and now I was training alongside them.

"Even the gaffer (David Gray) was intimidating to be near because I can remember playing in my garden and trying to recreate his goal and celebration from the Scottish Cup final with my brother!"

He did more than hold his own and earned the right to be on the same pitch as those Club legends.

At the end of a whirlwind campaign, he was chosen by the Academy coaches as their Player of the Year and that was an award he felt extremely privileged to receive.

He admitted: "It was a very proud moment for me. Last season was fantastic for me, although it was hectic at the same time.

"I want to keep pushing, working hard and developing my game. I cannot take anything for granted. Now that I've tasted first team football I want to play as much as I possibly can and the only way I'll do that is by impressing the coaches all over again."

Rory spent the first part of the season on a development loan with Spartans and will return to the Club in January.

PLAYER PROFILES

POSITION: GOALKEEPER

ERIN CLACHERS

Erin joined us on a season-long loan from Glasgow City. Despite making almost a century of appearances and picking up numerous winner's medals, she has spent a long time as a back-up to Lee Alexander. Clachers will be looking to make the number one berth her own this term and enjoy a consistent run of games to enable her development.

POSITION: GOALKEEPER

NOA SCHUMACHER

The young American will challenge Clachers for a starting berth this term. Until joining us this summer, Noa spent her entire career in her native America, progressing through the US college system. With California Baptist University, she won the Western Athletic Conference Goalkeeper of the Year award in 2023 and was included in the WAC Team of The Year.

POSITION: DEFENDER

LAUREN DORAN-BARR

Lauren made 34 appearances and scored twice for us last season. Her impressive performances saw her rewarded with a contract extension. She can play at full back or wing back and her boundless energy on the flanks has made her a firm fans' favourite. Her former clubs include Rangers, Stirling University and Motherwell.

POSITION: DEFENDER

POPPY LAWSON

Poppy was the only player to play over 3,000 minutes for Hibs Women last term. A reliable, consistent, combative, and natural-born leader; Lawson enjoyed a terrific season with us last year and made the right back position her own. The former Manchester United youngster is now in her third season with the Club and is contracted until the summer of 2026.

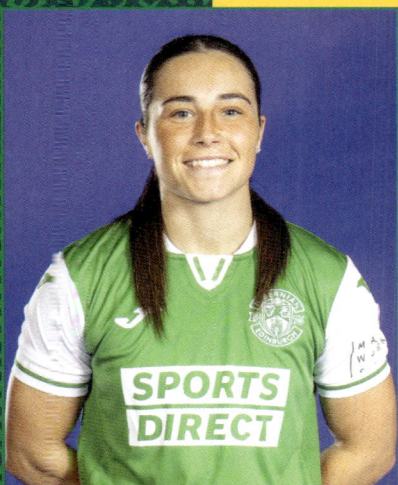

POSITION: DEFENDER

SIOBHAN HUNTER

Hunter is our longest-serving player, having made her debut for us back in August 2009 during a 3-1 victory over Forfar Farmington. A lifelong Hibee, Siobhan has shown remarkable loyalty to the Club over the years and her commitment to our cause has never wavered. The powerful centre back with a penchant for goals from spectacular long-range free kicks, has won seven major honours with the Club and represented us in European competition numerous times.

POSITION: DEFENDER

SHANNON LEISHMAN

Shannon, like Siobhan, is another long-serving Hibee, having come through the Academy and made her debut as a 16-year-old back in 2014 during a 2-2 draw with Rangers. A childhood Hibs supporter, Leishman has won two Scottish Cup and two SWPL Cups with Hibs. Last season, Shannon made her 150th appearance for us.

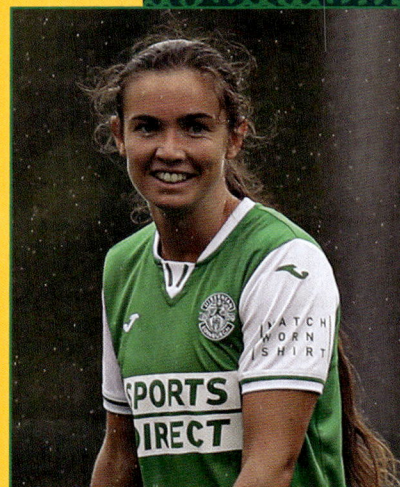

POSITION: DEFENDER

STACEY PAPADOPOULOS

The Australian joined us during the summer on a two-year deal from Western United. Stacey won a cup double in 2022 with Calder United before moving to Western United where she finished as runner-up in the Women's A-League. Papadopoulos has brought steadiness and energy to our defensive backline.

POSITION: DEFENDER

TEGAN BOWIE

Despite her relatively young age, Bowie plays with a maturity beyond her years and has grown into an instrumental player for us. A terrifically talented and tricky winger, she has shown time and time again she can cause any defence problems with her skill, movement, and speed. Tegan made 31 appearances for us last season, scoring once, and providing several assists.

POSITION: MIDFIELDER

ABBIE FERGUSON

The talented, young midfielder was regularly a stand-out performer for Grant Scott's side last season, contributing goals and assists consistently throughout the campaign. She arrived at the Club from Celtic, following a productive season-long loan at Partick Thistle where she caught Scott's eye. Ferguson once scored five goals in Scotland U19's 7-0 victory over Liechtenstein.

POSITION: MIDFIELDER

ELLIS NOTLEY

Ellis is another long-serving Hibee, having made over 200 appearances for the Club. She joined our Academy as a 13-year-old and quickly rose through the ranks before making her senior debut against Spartans in 2015. Notley's flexibility has allowed her to play in several positions. She has won five major honours with the Club and scored the opening goal in the 2018 SWPL Cup final vs Celtic, which we won 9-0.

POSITION: MIDFIELDER

MICHAELA MCALONIE

Despite her diminutive appearance, McAlonie is a tenacious battler and her will-to-win has made her a firm fans' favourite. The midfielder joined us from city rivals Spartans in 2021 and scored her first goal for us against her former side! Her performances regularly earn plaudits where her boundless energy and commitment shine through.

POSITION: MIDFIELDER

MYA CHRISTIE

After a string of impressive performances for Aberdeen, Grant Scott moved quickly to secure Mya's services when he was appointed Hibs boss. Having moved to us last summer, she quickly settled and made a telling contribution to the team where her determination and endeavour set the pace for her team-mates. Christie made 28 appearances last term, scoring once.

POSITION: MIDFIELDER

RACHAEL BOYLE

Rachael will be determined to make up for lost time this season having missed most of the last two seasons due to pregnancy then injury. A talismanic player, our captain has it all in her locker. A fierce competitor with the talent to unlock any defence with either a well-placed pass or a clinical finish. Rachael joined us from Aberdeen in 2016 and has won four trophies with us.

POSITION: MIDFIELDER

LINZI TAYLOR

The midfielder joined us during the close season on a two-year deal from Partick Thistle. She can play anywhere across the midfield and defensive lines. Linzi brings with her a wealth of experience and versatility. The former Scotland youth international has played for Celtic and Thistle in Scotland as well as sampling football abroad through spells in Iceland, Israel and Cyprus during her career to date.

POSITION: MIDFIELDER

KIRSTEN REILLY

The Musselburgh-born midfielder returned to the Club for a second spell during the summer when she penned a two-year deal. Kirsten won three major trophies with us first time around and she will be desperate to win even more. A childhood Hibs fan, Reilly arrives with a wealth of experience from successful spells with Bristol City, Rangers, and Crystal Palace.

POSITION: MIDFIELDER

CIARA GRANT

There were a few surprised onlookers when we tempted the Republic of Ireland international to swap Gorgie for Leith during the summer. The combative and dynamic midfielder joined us on a one-year contract. Grant was part of the Irish squad that reached the 2023 Women's World Cup in Australia and New Zealand and the Rangers team that won their first Scottish Women's Premier League title. She is also a qualified doctor, having picked up a degree in medicine from University College Dublin in 2017.

POSITION: FORWARD

EILIDH ADAMS

The prolific striker averaged a goal every 78 minutes last season – which was the best at the Club. Adams scored 14 goals in her 26 appearances before her campaign was brought to a premature end through injury. The Scotland youth international scored her first senior hat-trick in the 8-1 victory over Hamilton Academical in October 2023.

POSITION: FORWARD

KIRSTY MORRISON

Kirsty captained the side last season against Rangers as she marked the occasion of her 100th appearance for the Club by taking the armband. A reliable and intelligent forward, Morrison signed a one-year extension with us during the summer. She has now been with the Club for over ten years, and having missed a last part of the season through injury, she'll be looking to make up for lost time.

POSITION: FORWARD

LIA TWEEDIE

The powerful forward was consigned to just one starting appearance last term due to injury and the remarkable form of Jorian Baucom. Yet that didn't stop Lia scooping the Women's Goal of the Season award for her stunning effort against City rivals Hearts. Now in her second spell with the Club, Tweedie is closing in on her 50th goal for Hibs and she is keen to add to her six major honours.

POSITION: FORWARD

ROSIE LIVINGSTONE

Last season proved to be a frustrating one for Rosie as her campaign was continually disrupted by injury. Despite this, she still managed to make 19 appearances. The 19-year-old is highly regarded at the Club, and she has the potential to join the list of great players to have come through our Academy and gone on to make it to the highest level in women's football.

POSITION: FORWARD

KATHLEEN MCGOVERN

Like Grant, McGovern also crossed the city divide this summer when she joined us on a two-year deal after leaving Hearts. The Scotland youth international began her career with Celtic and was part of the Hoops side that won the 2021/22 SWPL Cup. She then moved to SC Sand in the Frauen Bundesliga before returning to Scotland. Kathleen netted a first half hat-trick on her Hibs debut against Boroughmuir Thistle.

SPOT THE BALL

Can you use your judgement and skill to spot which ball is the actual one from the match?

GO TO P60-61 FOR THE ANSWERS

WORDSEARCH

Can you find the words below in our 2007 League Cup final themed wordsearch?

A	Z	W	D	D	W	L	N	T	V	O	O	Q	E	Y	O	O	O	X	A	S	E	V	O	O
G	F	W	A	D	Q	P	A	I	K	R	E	K	A	T	T	I	H	W	N	E	V	E	T	S
Q	U	G	V	B	Q	O	T	T	L	I	N	O	O	G	C	U	B	I	O	B	Y	P	R	V
I	P	H	I	J	D	F	N	I	U	E	L	X	L	W	U	Z	V	N	Y	P	Q	O	O	S
J	H	N	D	Y	R	E	G	W	O	L	Z	M	Q	A	L	O	G	N	D	R	P	D	P	H
F	N	B	M	Z	R	E	S	G	O	G	W	U	A	W	G	Y	Q	E	W	F	T	I	H	E
P	F	M	U	G	G	O	H	S	I	R	H	C	E	R	N	F	X	R	Q	A	D	D	Y	L
H	U	R	R	V	O	L	R	C	A	Z	B	E	L	B	N	W	H	S	T	W	J	X	S	T
M	A	S	P	J	M	I	S	G	T	L	Q	T	T	I	E	O	O	S	V	J	S	D	E	O
L	E	E	H	N	G	O	U	E	D	E	A	J	T	E	E	M	C	R	V	U	R	N	P	N
Q	D	R	Y	I	O	Y	X	E	D	G	L	M	J	O	Z	N	U	K	B	Y	T	X	G	M
O	F	D	O	O	V	S	P	Y	R	A	J	F	B	N	C	P	C	A	Y	N	N	J	J	A
A	U	C	P	U	V	A	N	V	X	E	R	O	N	E	T	S	C	M	L	D	O	Q	E	R
D	U	R	K	R	A	P	N	E	D	P	M	A	H	E	N	L	X	H	Y	L	E	M	L	T
B	R	O	B	J	O	N	E	S	V	Q	C	A	P	N	V	J	U	Q	G	D	I	S	I	I
I	J	A	R	X	Q	Y	E	O	P	E	W	E	E	Y	C	E	E	V	D	V	N	U	N	S
K	Q	G	D	R	D	P	G	Z	H	R	T	O	E	T	R	O	T	L	Q	C	J	A	G	L
Q	W	J	F	Q	E	W	V	Q	E	Y	O	S	D	W	V	O	L	S	L	U	W	V	W	M
U	X	B	Q	G	U	H	B	X	M	M	X	U	S	O	Q	M	T	L	S	O	D	Q	Y	A
L	B	Z	V	M	T	C	P	K	E	G	M	I	L	I	N	C	X	C	I	A	U	J	V	O
A	F	K	A	P	V	K	B	D	C	X	X	A	S	E	W	K	W	Y	I	N	E	N	D	H
X	X	C	L	Y	G	C	B	M	Y	N	Q	U	M	L	R	E	C	N	I	V	S	C	X	G
Z	P	Q	Z	K	T	Z	Q	V	X	K	G	L	M	A	N	W	L	E	P	U	M	Z	X	F
D	O	K	C	B	J	N	N	A	C	C	M	N	I	V	E	K	C	P	S	Q	V	N	N	P
S	A	T	R	A	W	E	T	S	L	E	A	H	C	I	M	T	N	R	M	J	Q	N	X	C

Andy McNeil

Steven Whittaker

Shelton Martis

Chris Hogg

Kevin McCann

Rob Jones

David Murphy

Ivan Sproule

Merouane Zemmama

Scott Brown

Guillaume Beuzelin

Lewis Stevenson

Abdessalam Benjelloun

Steven Fletcher

Simon Brown

Michael Stewart

John Collins

Hampden Park

Kilmarnock

Winners

Victory Parade

Trophy

GO TO
P60-61
FOR THE
ANSWERS

COMING HOME: KIRSTEN REILLY

Kirsten Reilly admits the lure of coming home to Hibs was too strong and she couldn't be happier to be back.

The 29-year-old midfielder returned to the Club this summer for a second spell, having previously played for us during the 2018 and 2019 campaigns. She is once again reunited with boss Grant Scott, having played for him before at Heart of Midlothian, Stirling University and of course, Hibs.

Kirsten's first spell at the Club was certainly a successful one as she picked up winner's medals in three domestic cup competitions as well as representing Hibs in the UEFA Women's Champions League. The attraction of coming back to her first love and trying to win silverware was something she couldn't turn down.

"I'm absolutely buzzing to be back," commented Kirsten about her return. "It's great to be back, wearing that famous green shirt and playing for Hibs once again.

"I've been a Hibs supporter my whole life and I come from a family of passionate Hibees, who are all equally as excited as I am.

"When Grant called me and asked if I would be interested in coming back home, obviously being back in Scotland was great but being back at Hibs was the biggest pulling point for me.

"There was no easier decision. I was a season ticket holder from a very young age and grew up supporting the Club. It's all I've ever known, and to play professionally for Hibs is a dream come true."

Despite being away from Easter Road for five years as her career took her to Bristol City, Rangers and Crystal Palace, Hibernian Women continued to be on her mind.

She revealed: "The Club have never been far from my thoughts since I left in 2019, and when I could I'd be up the road to watch the games. Other times, I'd watch the games on TV or on the Club's YouTube channel.

"My family would sometimes go to the games when they couldn't come to mine down south.

"I feel like I have continued to have a connection to the team whilst I was away, and because Ellis [Notley] is my best friend, she's kept me in the loop with the goings on at the Club."

When it comes to Edinburgh derbies, Reilly is no stranger, having represented both Hibs and Hearts. The final match of her first spell with us was against the Jambos with Hibs running out 7-1 winners.

In the years since, the derby has grown much more competitive, and in recent seasons we have witnessed record attendances at Easter Road and Tynecastle.

"That was the first fixture I looked for when they came out," admitted Kirsten.

"As I said I've supported Hibs all my life, so I know how big the derbies are. To be involved in them now, as the women's game continues to grow, is really exciting."

Like so many Hibees, our 2016 Scottish Cup victory over Rangers ranks as one of the best days of our lives and for Kirsten, it was no different. In fact, when it came to choosing a squad number when she initially joined us, she chose one with extra significance.

"When I signed for Hibs the first time, my brother told me I had to take the squad number 32, so I did, and I've stuck with it.

"Well, not always, when I signed for Rangers, I did quietly drop it for number eight as I didn't think that would go down well if I didn't!"

Last season Reilly was converted into a right-back at Crystal Palace, but she admits she's happier in the middle of the park where she can have a greater influence.

"I've played under Grant a few times now and I know how he operates and what he wants from his players.

"When we started talking and he told me there was an opportunity to come home, I thought it was the perfect time for me.

"I've enjoyed my time in England, although I was playing right back which I don't think is my best position.

"So, I'm happy to be back playing centre-mid again and to be helping the team in what I consider the core area of the pitch.

"It's a big season for us and we want to get more points to finish higher up the table than the last couple of years.

"Personally, I want to be contributing goals, setting up goals for my team-mates and helping the youngsters in our squad, because we have a young team at Hibs."

WHY I LOVE HIBS...

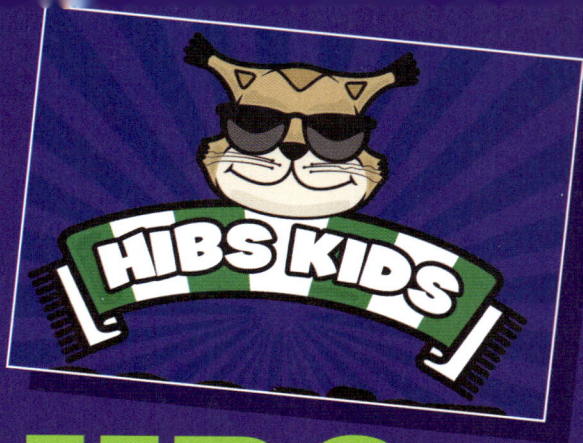

We caught up with Hibs Kid, Daniel McBrierty, aged nine, to discuss his Hibstory and love for the Club.

Who do you attend games with?

"I go with my dad. I have been going to Easter Road since I was two. Both my grandads and loads of my dad's friends go, sometimes my cousin too. They are always having a laugh with me and asking what the score will be. There is always a big group of us that go to the games. I love being part of it all."

What is your match-day routine?

"I play on a Saturday morning, so after scoring plenty goals and getting a win, we rush to get to Easter Road. I get changed into my Hibs gear quickly and then off we go to Leith, listening to some Hibs podcasts. I go into the Albion Bar to watch the lunchtime game on TV, and I have a steak pie and Irn Bru for lunch. Sometimes I see some of the players and ask them to sign my autograph book and get photos. I do get excited wanting the game to start, so I'm always asking when it is time to go to our seats."

Can you remember your first game?

"I was just about to turn two and, although I don't remember it, it was against St Mirren when we got presented with the Championship trophy. My mum and dad tell me I was out of control in wanting to go onto the pitch and play. I wouldn't take no for an answer, so we had to leave at half time! Apparently, I was not happy when I heard the cheer from the stadium for Grant Holt's goal and wanted to go back."

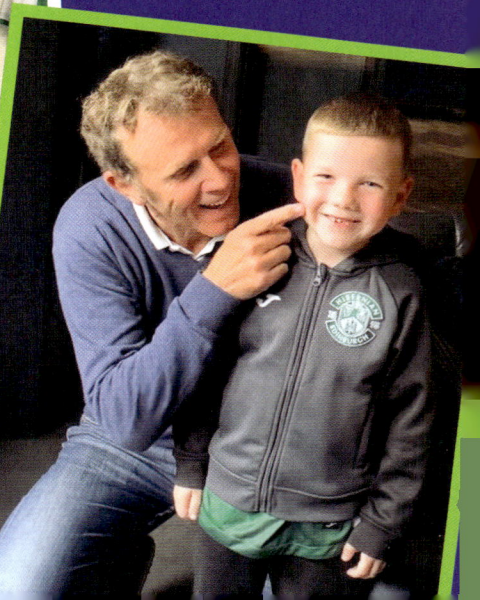

What has been your favourite Hibs game you've attended?

"Aston Villa in Birmingham. My dad said I was too wee to go to Switzerland with him, but promised if we got through against Luzern, he would take me to Villa Park. It was brilliant. It was a massive party before the game and I was leading the singing, up on people's shoulders and getting loads of pictures before the game."

Who was your first Hibs hero?

"Christian Doidge. My first away game was in Perth against St Johnstone when Doidgey scored his hat-trick. After that it was only his name I wanted on my shirts. I was lucky to meet him lots. He was always asking about how my football was going and asking how many goals I had scored. He also gave me one of his shirts which is in a frame up in my bedroom."

Who is your current favourite player?

"Josh Campbell. He is my favourite player because he's an Edinburgh boy, Hibs fan, works hard always and scores goals like me."

And your favourite former Hibee?

"My favourite is Franck Sauzée. My dad says he was the best player he has seen play at Hibs. I got to meet him when he came back to Easter Road a few seasons ago and he was a really nice man."

What is your favourite goal?

"Martin Boyle's injury time goal against Hearts. I went mental celebrating it."

What has been your best moment supporting Hibs?

"Being a mascot against Celtic. I got to lead the team onto the pitch with David Marshall. All my family were there. It was so noisy. Everyone was cheering and clapping. I loved it. I got to meet all the players from Hibs and a couple of Celtic players. I want to walk out onto the pitch as a player when I'm older."

What do you want to be when you grow up?

"I want to be Hibs captain and win the Scottish Cup, score loads of goals and get lots of wins against Hearts."

MEMORABILIA
MATCH PROGRAMMES

It was once the matchday staple for many and the only form of news that came unfiltered directly from the Club.

These days, the match programme is a dying art with many clubs (including ourselves) no longer producing them.

The advent of the internet, social media and access to the most up-to-date news electronically as soon as it breaks, meant that there was no longer an appetite for traditional media.

Out of date almost as soon as they were printed, the rising costs and declining sales meant they were no longer viable.

Programmes began to be mass produced at games all over the country following the Second World War (having been sporadic before 1946) and

for almost 80 years their place in the matchday itinerary for many was solidified.

At Hibs, we believe that we adapt to the changing requirements of supporters and although we no longer produce programmes, we do publish a magazine – Hibernian Quarterly – that we feel is a better fit for today's supporter.

It's packed full of unique and insightful content that fans would never find in traditional programmes.

That said, memorabilia remains important to many, and in this year's Annual, we look back at the changing face of match programmes at our Club.

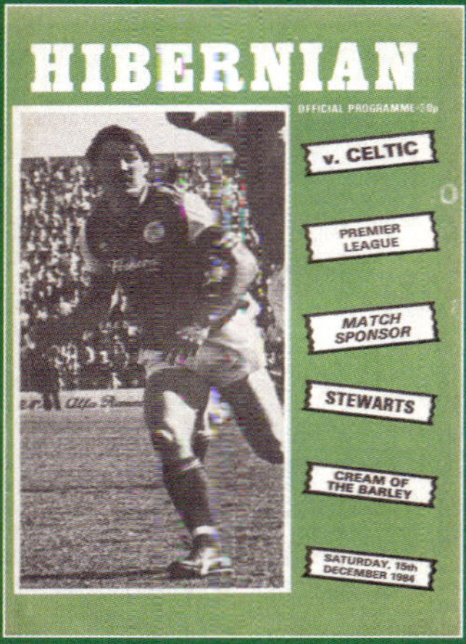
HIBERNIAN
OFFICIAL PROGRAMME 50p
v. CELTIC
PREMIER LEAGUE
MATCH SPONSOR
STEWARTS
CREAM OF THE BARLEY
SATURDAY, 15th DECEMBER 1984

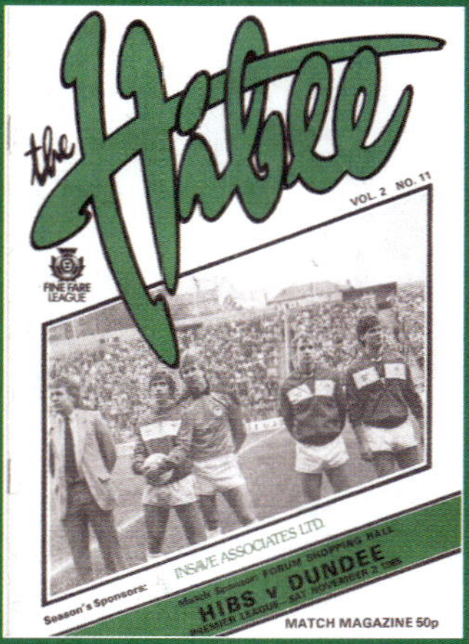
the Hibee
VOL. 2 NO. 11
FINE FARE LEAGUE
Season's Sponsors: INSAVE ASSOCIATES LTD.
HIBS v DUNDEE
MATCH MAGAZINE 50p

Hibernian
FOOTBALL CLUB LIMITED
Hibernian v Rangers
£1

Hibernian
FOOTBALL CLUB
£1.00
Hibernian v Heart of Midlothian

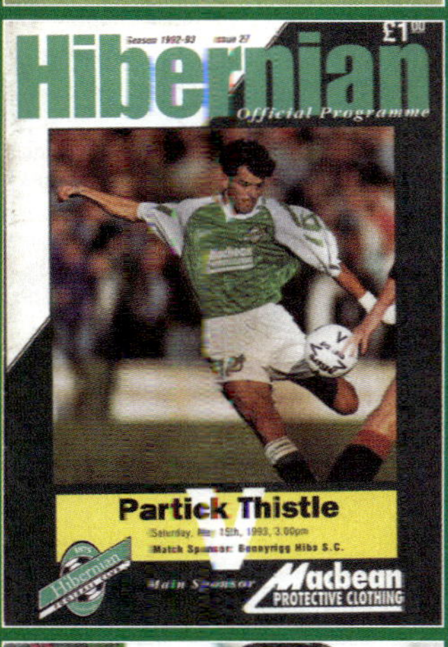
Season 1992-93
Issue 27
£1.00
Hibernian
Official Programme
Partick Thistle
Macbean
PROTECTIVE CLOTHING

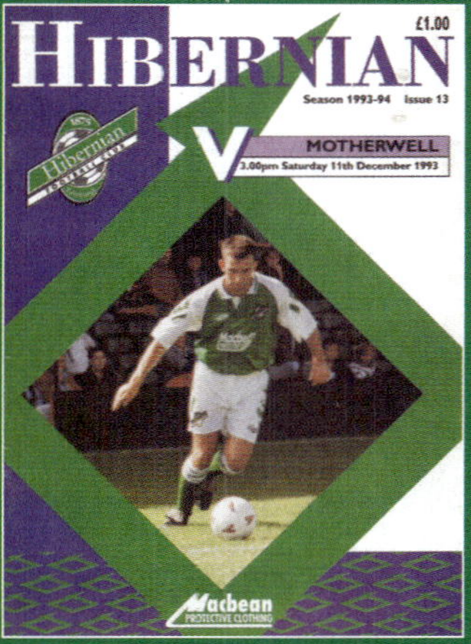
£1.00
HIBERNIAN
Season 1993-94 Issue 13
V
MOTHERWELL
3.00pm Saturday 11th December 1993
Macbean
PROTECTIVE CLOTHING

1994-95
Issue 15
Hibernian
Aberdeen
Bell's League Championship Premier Division
CALOR Gas
Mitre

FOOTBALL CLUB
£1.00
Hibernian
MIDDLESBROUGH
CALOR Gas
Mitre

FOOTBALL CLUB
KILMARNOCK
3.00pm Saturday
23 August 1997
£1.50
JM
Carlsberg
Mitre

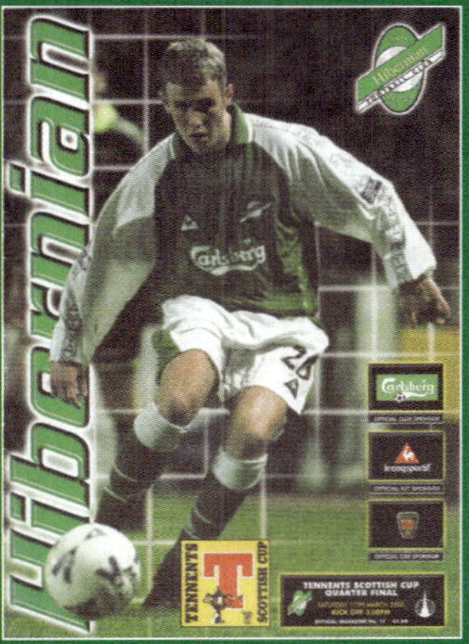
Hibernian
TENNENTS
SCOTTISH CUP
Carlsberg

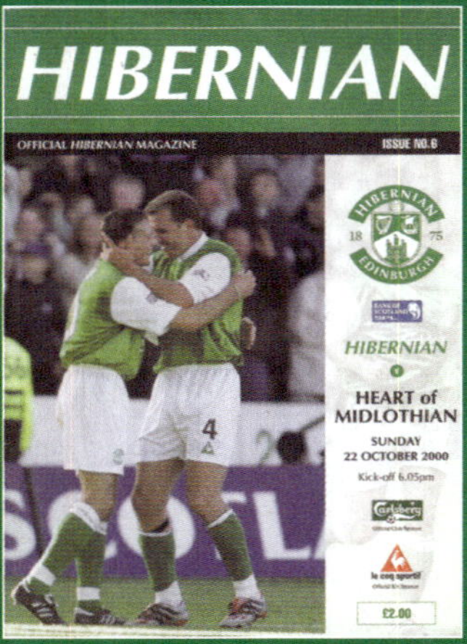
HIBERNIAN
OFFICIAL HIBERNIAN MAGAZINE
ISSUE NO.6
HIBERNIAN
HEART of MIDLOTHIAN
SUNDAY
22 OCTOBER 2000
£2.00

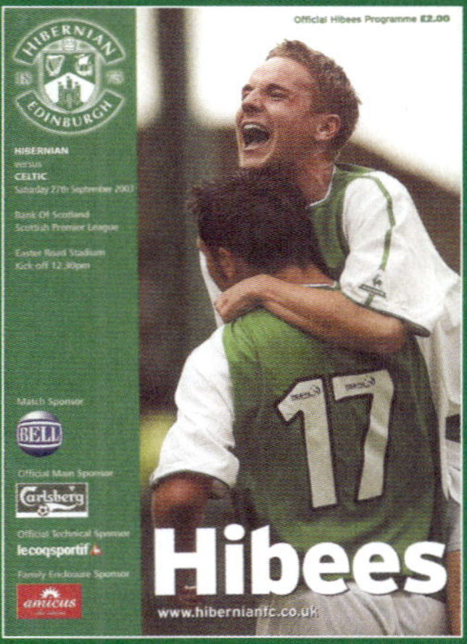
Official Hibees Programme £2.00
HIBERNIAN
EDINBURGH
CELTIC
Carlsberg
17
Hibees
www.hibernianfc.co.uk

HIBERNIAN F.C.
MATCHDAY MAGAZINE £2
HIBERNIAN v LIVINGSTON
BANK OF SCOTLAND
WHYTE & MACKAY

INTERTOTO CUP
CARLING
HOME

GOALMOUTH
THE OFFICIAL HIBERNIAN MATCHDAY GUIDE ISSUE 01 • £2.00
READY TO GO
HOMEWOOD FLOORING

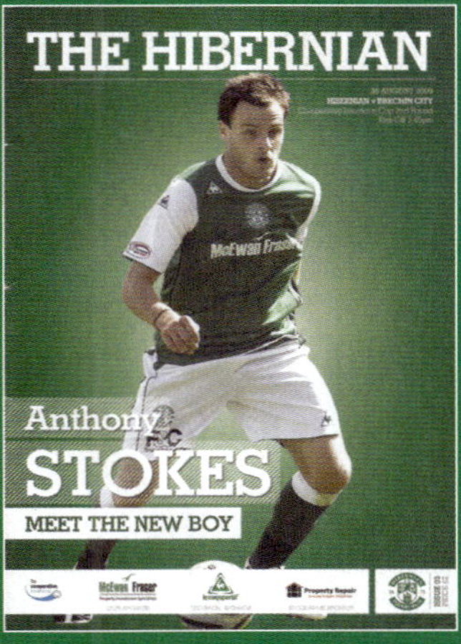
THE HIBERNIAN
Anthony
STOKES
MEET THE NEW BOY

HIBERNIAN COMMUNITY FOUNDATION

Hibernian Community Foundation reflects the values of the Club when it was first formed, using funds raised to support the local population. We take a look at six amazing initiatives the foundation is using to benefit our community today.

Ron Gordon Football Challenge

The Ron Gordon Football Challenge was a monumental success, showcasing the power of sports in fostering community spirit as funds were raised for our Community Meals programme directly from Hibernian Training Centre.

Christmas Lunch

Over 300 people attended the Christmas Lunch hosted at Easter Road Stadium. We also delivered food to 170 people across 90 locations, with over 65% of the home drop-offs being made to community members living alone.

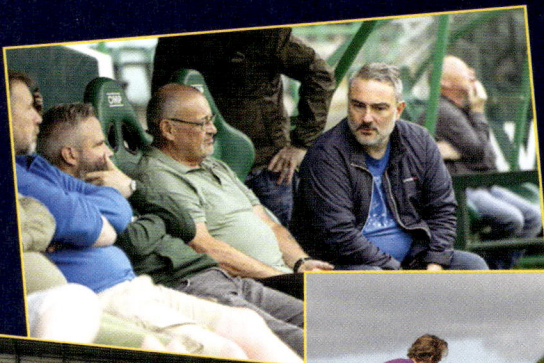

The Changing Room/Supporting Our Supporters

The Changing Room promotes mental health and wellbeing for both men and women through the power of the beautiful game. Supporting Our Supporters is a monthly mental health drop-in run by HCF volunteers. These gatherings are well attended, with special guests delivering talks that are entertaining, informative and inspirational.

Hibernian Community Choir

In partnership with Leod Music, our latest initiative, the choir helps individuals build positivity and confidence, making new friends, taking part in fun events and being part of something new.

Lunch Club/Pitch to Plate

Hosting two lunches a week in partnership with Empty Kitchens Full Hearts, providing a hot two-course meal and allowing individuals the opportunity to socialise with friends, family and make new friends within our community. Pitch to Plate is a multi-cultural meal that takes place on the last Tuesday of every month.

Ron Gordon's Extra Time

Ron Gordon's Extra Time gives parents and carers 'extra time' to do whatever's most important in their lives. This could be spending a few more hours at work, spending time to enhance their employment prospects, or looking after their own mental health and well-being.

SPOT THE DIFFERENCE

GO TO P60-61 FOR THE ANSWERS

Using your observational skills, can you seek out and find the eight differences between the two images from our Premier Sports Cup clash with Queen's Park earlier this season?

BRING ON THE SPANIARDS BY THE SCORE!

Despite reaching the semi-final stage of the inaugural European Cup, it would be five years before the Club were back in competitive action on the continent.

Hugh Shaw's team was almost unrecognisable to the side that faced Stade de Reims.

Our renowned forward-line *'The Famous Five'* were now a distant memory, although Bobby Johnstone had returned to the Club following a spell at Manchester City.

We relied heavily on the goals of youngster Joe Baker; a breathtaking marksman whose exploits in front of a goal would struggle to be matched by a comic-strip character.

Despite his heroic goal haul, we were toiling on the domestic front. Our seventh place finish the season before was our best for four years and we were now flirting with relegation from Division 1.

The Inter-Cities Fairs Cup offered us relief from our domestic woes and the first-round draw paired us with Lausanne-Sports from Switzerland.

Yet, before the players could look out for their passports, the Swiss team withdrew. They believed they didn't have a team good enough to face us and therefore didn't believe there was any point in turning up and suffering a heavy defeat.

As a result of this, we were awarded a 'walkover' and were in the quarter-finals without having kicked a ball. The draw couldn't have been more glamourous as we were paired with Spanish superstars Barcelona in a mouth-watering final eight tie.

The Catalans were as famous back then as they are now and were a team revered throughout the game.

The first leg had been scheduled for mid-December at Easter Road, only for heavy fog to force the referee into a postponement. It wasn't just the weather that cleared overnight, so too had the Spaniards as they reneged on an agreement to play the contest 24 hours later and headed home.

54

Two weeks later, we arrived in Spain only to be denied our prearranged access to the Nou Camp. The gamesmanship of the Spaniards backfired spectacularly when our players did eventually get out onto the pitch.

Shaw's approach was to play a brand of cavalier football where attack was the best form of defence.

David took the game to Goliath, and in the opening exchanges we raced into a 2-0 lead thanks to goals from Baker and Johnny MacLeod.

Barcelona was the best club side in Europe, if not the world, and had been expected to coast to victory against an opponent that was flirting with relegation back home.

Eventually, they settled and played the type of football they were renowned for. Their constant pressure paid off when Sandor Kocsis, the legendary Hungarian international, scored either side of the interval to restore parity.

Most expected them to go on and claim a comfortable win, only for our boys to once more stun the home support with another quick-fire double through Tommy Preston and Baker.

For the second time that evening, Barcelona were trailing by two goals and staring straight into the face of defeat that would send shockwaves around Europe.

With six minutes remaining, Kocsis completed his hat-trick when he stabbed the ball home before Evaristo de Macedo scored at the death to snatch a famous victory from our grasp.

It would be nearly two whole months before the second leg in Edinburgh, and unsurprisingly, a bumper crowd packed into Easter Road to set a record attendance for a European match in Edinburgh.

After being given the run-around by Baker in the first leg, the Barcelona defenders did their best to prevent a repeat and he was the recipient of numerous crunching tackles early on.

Yet the youngster was unfazed and rose above the Barca keeper to meet MacLeod's cross to head us in front. The goal not only sparked delirium on the terraces, it shocked Barcelona into life, as goals from Eulogio Martinez and Kocsis turned the match on its head before the break.

Shooting down the slope, we battered their defence with renewed vigour as the visitors resorted to increasingly aggressive measures.

The Barcelona players must have felt that they were in the path of an unstoppable tsunami as we flooded forward in waves.

With 16 minutes remaining, Preston headed in to level the tie once more before we were awarded a penalty kick in the dying embers after MacLeod was scythed down, sparking scenes of infamy.

The German match official was immediately surrounded by the Barcelona players, and he was pushed around so much that the police had to step in to protect him and restore order.

When it was, Bobby Kinloch stepped forward and duly dispatched his kick to win the tie and secure one of the biggest results in Scottish football history.

Our journey would end at the semi-final stage after three incredible matches with Italian giants Roma, who would go on to win the competition.

INSIDE EASTER ROAD WITH DEREK WHITE

We like to take supporters behind the scenes at Easter Road and speak to some of the unsung heroes around the Club. This year we speak to Derek White, Head of Football Operations, about his role with us.

Derek, can you take us through your background and how you ended up at Hibs?

Well, I played with Livingston from U13 up to reserve team football. Whilst I was in the Academy, I volunteered on matchdays helping out. A vacancy came up for supporter liaison officer and I was approached about doing it. I did that on a voluntary basis for about a year or so. At a club like Livi, you begin to get handed different jobs and that led to the media role, doing things like setting up interviews, press conferences, dealing with the national media and co-ordinating live TV games. Over time it then progressed into football operations and co-ordinating team travel, overnight stays, match organisation, stewarding and a lot more. It really snowballed!

How big an impact did Covid play on your role?

I had just been appointed Club Secretary when Covid hit. Myself and a couple of other staff members were leading on the Covid procedures, policies and measures that were required to be put in place. It was a hectic time. We had to draft new processes and put them in place which involved a lot of operational tweaking for things like social distancing, the return of supporters, ticketing – in terms of splitting groups up or having social bubbles – things that were brand new to us all. Covid played a huge part of my development, and it was a long 18 months.

How does your role at Hibs differ from the one you left at Livi?

As I mentioned before, because of the type of club Livi are, there are fewer staff and I had a wide-ranging role, across so many different departments. At Hibs, I am restricted to the football department and that allows me to be more in-depth and really focus in on what matters. My scope may be narrower, however there is greater demand and more complexity to it.

How would you describe your key activities?

I see myself as having six key activities. They are: *matchday operations* – everything that surrounds getting the team to and from a matchday. *Training ground facility management* – making sure the training ground is in a suitable state and that we are constantly improving it. *Contract and transfer management* – drafting contracts, transfer agreements and working with lawyers. *SPFL and SFA compliance* – ensuring we follow rules and regulations. *UEFA and Club licensing* – the Club's annual submission and, finally, *Player Care* – helping relocate players to Edinburgh, supporting them with property, cars, and general support.

What does a typical matchday look like for you?

Matchdays are usually quiet for me because our hard work is done in the days building up to it. For away games, myself and Phil Kidd, our football operations co-ordinator, will be around to make sure everything goes smoothly. Phil will go to the team hotel and if there are any issues, he will deal with them. I will go to the stadium early with the kit manager, so if there are any issues there, such as the pitch isn't playable or security concerns, then I'm there as a point of contact. Generally, on matchday we are there for any last-minute issues that crop up.

You're heavily involved in the planning of pre-season training camps. Can you give us an insight into the level of planning and detail that goes into them?

At the start of planning, I sit down with the various departments, and we review the previous camp. What did and didn't go well? What do we need next time? The coaching staff will look for two full-sized pitches with several portable goals. Medical will want a good-sized room, with a bed and plenty of ice. Head of physical performance will want a high-quality gym with x, y and z equipment. So, I collate all this then work with my contacts to say this is our requirement. Around November time, we go and visit a couple of proposed locations where I will assess their facilities against our criteria, taking photos and presenting back to the coaching staff. I go over our options, the cost of those and offer my opinion. A final decision is made around Christmas time, and it's booked in January. The next six months are used to decide how many people are travelling, how many flights are booked, pulling together menus, how much water is needed, hiring a minivan. It's a gradual build up to the trip and nothing is left to the last minute. There's a lot of detail that goes into a trip that goes unnoticed by those even on the trip, including players, but it is all worthwhile.

What is the best part of working for Hibs?

Easy, the environment and the people. At Hibs we have so many good people that really want to do well for the Club. Coming in each day doesn't feel like work because you know when you go into Hibs Training Centre that there will be a buzz about the place. The environment and culture set at the Club – from the top down – is one of the best that I have worked in or will likely ever work in.

CLUB CONTACT INFORMATION

Stadium Address:
Easter Road Stadium,
12 Albion Place,
Edinburgh, EH7 5QG

Email: club@hibernianfc.co.uk

Telephone
0131 661 2159

Social Media
Facebook: Hibernian Football Club Official
Instagram: HibernianFootballClub
Instagram: Hibernianwomen
Twitter: @HibernianFC
Twitter: @HibernianWomen
LinkedIn: Hibernian FC
YouTube: @Hibernian FC
Website: www.hibernianfc.co.uk

Ticket Office
Email: tickets@hibernianfc.co.uk
Opening Hours:
Monday to Friday, 10am-5pm
(via email and telephone)
Monday – Friday 10am – 4pm in person

Clubstore
Email: info@hiberniandirect.co.uk
Telephone: 0131 656 7078

Hospitality
Email: hospitality@hibernianfc.co.uk

Hibernian Community Foundation
Email: info@hiberniancf.org
Telephone: 0131 656 7062

CLUB HONOURS

MEN

Scottish League
Winners (4): 1902/03, 1947/48, 1950/51, 1951/52
Runners-up (6): 1896/97, 1946/47, 1949/50, 1952/53, 1973/74, 1974/75

Scottish Cup
Winners (3): 1886/87, 1901/02, 2015/16
Runners-up (12): 1895/96, 1913/14, 1922/23, 1923/24, 1946/47, 1957/58, 1971/72, 1978/79, 2000/01, 2011/12, 2012/13, 2020/21

League Cup
Winners (3): 1972/73, 1991/92, 2006/07
Runners-up (8): 1950/51, 1968/69, 1974/75, 1985/86, 1993/94, 2003/04, 2015/16, 2021/22

Scottish League (tier two)
Winners (6): 1893/94, 1894/95, 1932/33, 1980/81, 1998/99, 2016/17
Runners-up (1): 2014/15

Drybrough Cup
Winners (2): 1972, 1973

Summer Cup
Winners (2): 1941, 1964

Southern League Cup:
Winners (1): 1943/44

SFA Youth Cup
Winners (3): 1991/92, 2008/09, 2017/18
Runners-up (2): 1989/90, 1990/91

WOMEN

Scottish Women's Premier League
Winners (3): 2003/04, 2005/06, 2006/07
Runners-up (9): 2002/03, 2004/05, 2007/08, 2013*, 2015*, 2016*, 2017*, 2018*, 2019*

Scottish Cup
Winners (8): 2002/03, 2004/05, 2006/07, 2007/08, 2010*, 2016*, 2017*, 2018*
Runners-up (4): 2011*, 2013*, 2015*, 2019*

Scottish Women's Premier League Cup
Winners (7): 2004/05, 2007/08, 2011*, 2016*, 2017*, 2018*, 2019*
Runners-up (5): 2006/07, 2009*, 2014*, 2015*, 2022/23

Between 2009-2020 women's football switched to a summer league, meaning fixtures were completed across one calendar year.

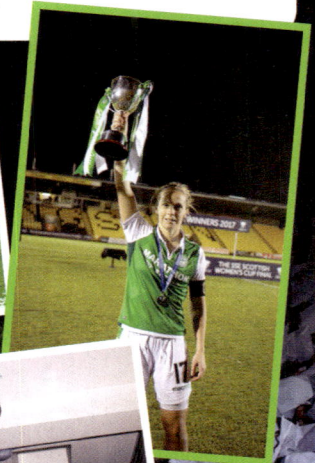

TIME FOR HEROES

QUIZ ANSWERS

P26. WHO AM I?

| Chris Cadden | Joe Newell | Josh Campbell | Eilidh Adams |

P30-31. SEASON QUIZ

1. St Johnstone, 10-0
2. Aberdeen, 2-0 at Pittodrie
3. Ten clean sheets
4. Katie Fraine
5. England at Wembley Stadium
6. Hertha Berlin
7. Jorian Baucom (x2), Eilidh Adams (x2), Abbie Ferguson and Michaela McAlonie
8. 83 seconds
9. Nine 2-2 draws in all competitions
10. Jamie McCluskey (16 years and 79 days old)
11. Heart of Midlothian
12. 28 goals
13. Motherwell
14. Joe Newell (12 yellow cards)
15. Jordan Obita

P44. SPOT THE BALL

```
A Z W D D W L N T V O O Q E Y O O O X A S E V O O
G F W A D Q P A I K R E K A T T I H W N E V E T S
Q U G V B Q O T T L I N O O G C U B I O B Y P R V
I P H I J D F N I U E L X L W U Z V N Y P Q O O S
J H N D Y R E G W O L Z M Q A L O G N D R P D P H
F N B M Z R E S G O G W U A W G Y Q E W F T I H E
P F M U G G O H S I R H C E R N F X R Q A D D Y L
H U R R V O L R C A Z B E L B N W H S T W J X S T
M A S P J M I S G T L Q T T I E O O S V J S D E O
L E E H N G O U E D E A J T E E M C R V U R N P N
Q D R Y I O Y X E D G L M J O Z N U K B Y T X G M
O F D O O V S P Y R A J F B N C A Y N N J J A
A U C P U V A N V X E R O N E T S C M L D O Q E R
D U R K R A P N E D P M A H E N L X H Y L E M L T
B R O B J O N E S V Q C A P N V J U Q G D I S I I
I J A R X Q Y E O P E W E E Y C E E V D V N U N S
K Q G D R D P G Z H R T O E T R O T L Q C J A G L
Q W J F Q E W V Q E Y O S D W V O L S L U W V W M
U X B Q G H B X M M X U S O Q M T L S O D Q Y A
L B Z V M T C P K E G M I L I N C X C I A U J V O
A F K A P V K B D C X X A S E W K W Y I N E N D H
X X C L Y G C B M Y N Q U M L R E C N I V S C X G
Z P Q Z K T Z Q V X K G L M A N W L E P U M Z X F
D O K C B J N N A C C M N I V E K C P S Q V N N P
S A T R A W E T S L E A H C I M T N R M J Q N X C
```

P53. SPOT THE DIFFERENCE

61

WHERE IS SUNSHINE THE LEITH LYNX?